I0805164

Animals in My World

CATS AND DOGS!

Andrea Palmer

HABA®

PowerKiDS press.

NEW YORK

Published in 2018 by The Rosen Publishing Group, Inc.
29 East 21st Street, New York, NY 10010

First Edition

Editor: Melissa Raé Shofner
Book Design: Michael Flynn

Photo Credits: Cover vvita/Shutterstock.com; p. 5 Layne Kennedy/Corbis Documentary/Getty Images; p. 6 vladimir salman/Shutterstock.com; p. 9 Jozef_Culak/Shutterstock.com; p. 10 DavidTB/Shutterstock.com; pp. 13, 24 (sheep) Nikolina Mrakovic/Shutterstock.com; p. 14 Ulrike Welsch/Science Source/Getty Images; p. 17 Alexandru Todor/Shutterstock.com; p. 18 valenmar96/Shutterstock.com; p. 21 Fernández Freire/EyeEm/Getty Images; p. 22 Grigorita Ko/Shutterstock.com; p. 24 (mice) Nick Vorobey/Shutterstock.com; p. 24 (rabbit) Leena Robinson/Shutterstock.com.

Cataloging-in-Publication Data

Names: Palmer, Andrea.
Title: Cats and dogs! / Andrea Palmer.
Description: New York : PowerKids Press, 2018. | Series: Animals in my world | Includes index.
Identifiers: ISBN 9781538321898 (pbk.) | ISBN 9781538321911 (library bound) | ISBN 9781538321904 (6 pack)
Subjects: LCSH: Cats–Juvenile literature. | Dogs–Juvenile literature. | Farm life–Juvenile literature.
Classification: LCC SF442.P35 2018 | DDC 636.8–dc23

Manufactured in the United States of America

CPSIA Compliance Information: Batch #BS17PK: For Further Information contact Rosen Publishing, New York, New York at 1-800-237-9932

Please visit: www.rosenpublishing.com and www.habausa.com

CONTENTS

Cats and Dogs

Cats can live on the farm. Dogs can live on the farm, too. How are dogs and cats the same? How are they different? Can cats and dogs be friends?

Soft Fur

Cats have soft fur. Their fur can be many colors. Some cats have stripes. Some cats have spots. Cats lick their fur. This keeps their fur clean.

Dogs have soft fur, too. Their fur can be many colors. Some dogs have spots. Some dogs have long fur. The farmer brushes the dogs' fur.

Jobs on the Farm

Cats have a job on the farm. Their job is to keep mice away. Cats chase mice in the field. They also chase mice in the barn.

Dogs have a job on the farm, too. They watch the sheep in the field. They keep the sheep safe. Dogs herd the sheep into the barn.

Eating and Playing

Cats and dogs both drink water. Cats like to eat cat food. Sometimes they drink milk. Dogs like to eat dog chow. They like to chew on bones.

Cats like to sleep a lot. They lie in the sun to keep warm. Cats like to chase mice and birds. They can run fast. They're good at jumping, too.

Dogs like to chase small animals. Sometimes they chase rabbits. Dogs can run fast. They love to bark, too. Dogs like to nap after they play.

Getting Along

Dogs and cats get into fights. Dogs will bark at cats. Cats will hiss at dogs. They chase each other around the farm. Cats will climb to get away.

Cats and dogs don't always fight. Sometimes they play together on the farm. They run in the field. They hide in the barn. Cats and dogs can be good friends.

WORDS TO KNOW

mice

rabbit

sheep

INDEX